clueless evangelism

how to share your faith
when you haven't got a clue

clueless evangelism

how to share your faith when you haven't got a clue

by michael kast

illustrated by keith locke

EMPOWERED
YOUTH PRODUCTS

Standard Publishing
Cincinnati, Ohio

Table of Contents

Cover Illustration by Keith Locke
Cover design by Dina Sorn
Edited by Dale Reeves

Library of Congress Cataloging-in-Publication Data:
Kast, Michael, 1966-
  Clueless evangelism : how to share your faith when you haven't got a clue / by Michael Kast ; illustrated by Keith Locke.
     p. cm.
  ISBN 0-7847-0612-3
  1. Evangelistic work--Study and teaching--Activity programs. 2. Junior high school students--Religious life. 3. Church group work with teenagers. I. Title.
  BV3796.K37   1997
  248'.5'0712--dc21   96-48941
                          CIP

The Standex Publishing Company, Cincinnati, Ohio.
A Division of Standex International Corporation.

04 03 02 01 00 99 98 97

5 4 3 2 1

This four-lesson series is aimed at junior high students, designed to teach them how they can bring their friends into a lifelong relationship with Jesus Christ. This is not a quick fix or step-by-step guide, but it *is* a plan—if you take the time to teach it to your kids—that really works. There are four lessons and one bonus session designed specifically for introducing new students to God.

When most people think of junior high students, they cringe and remember all the problems they experienced as an early adolescent. Often we don't give junior high students enough credit. I am reminded of that each time the Olympics roll around and the hopes and successes of entire countries are pinned on a 13-year-old gymnast or a 14-year-old figure skater. Junior high students are capable of doing some very incredible things.

Junior high students have the potential for sharing the gospel with their friends in a very unashamed way, unlike their older high school peers. These kids will talk about God and church in an open and honest way that is rare in the world today. Most of them are beginning to think for themselves, although some parents would not agree. And they begin to question what has been taught them. This is great because it gives them the opportunity to build a relationship with God on their own, rather than just adopt the faith of their parents or Sunday school teacher.

Junior high kids are also full of energy. Just ask someone who has worked with them for a short time and they'll agree. If we can direct this energy, they can seriously impact the world for Jesus Christ. The problem in the past has been that we, as youth leaders, have fired them up to save the world. It could have happened at a week of camp, a powerful retreat or on a mission trip. The kids returned and set off for school—ready to witness to everyone they would meet. Then, they hit the front steps of their campus and began to realize how big the task really was. So they simply didn't make any attempt at all. Then they felt like failures. They struggled with feelings of guilt. They experienced that all-too-common disease of going-home-after-the-camp-or-retreat-to-save-the-world-and-crashing-and-burning. There *is* a more effective method.

This study is designed to be used as a four-session elective to be taught to your core, solid Christian students. Each lesson is intended to teach them how to reach one person. They will choose one person that they want to point to Jesus Christ. This individual becomes their "point person"—the person that they are praying for and working on leading to God. Your students will learn: how to develop purposeful relationships; how to prepare and use their testimony; how to begin a conversation with their point person that leads into a discussion about God; and how to lead their friend into a relationship with God.

The next step is getting these new, baby Christians plugged into a ministry that will help them grow. Effective junior high ministry needs to include four basic elements. The first level is outreach; the second level is education; the third is worship; and the last level is discipleship. Most youth groups do a good job with education (Sunday school) and discipleship (youth group). Yet, many youth ministries struggle with outreach (usually putt-putt) and worship (adult worship not necessarily on the level of the students). The worst thing that anyone could do would be to have their students bring someone to Christ and then leave them there with no opportunity for growth.

These sessions are designed for you to teach your students how to lead their friends into a relationship with Jesus Christ. There are three sections to each lesson: **Open It Up**—designed to introduce your students to today's lesson; **Get Into It**—designed to get them into today's Scripture; and **Take It With You**—designed to help them apply today's lesson. Each of these sections presents more than one option for you to choose as learning activities. These are represented by the 👑 icon.

The purpose of the bonus session is to provide an outreach event to which your students can bring their "point people." It is flexible and will work with a group from 10 to 500 or more. I have seen this same style of program work in both small churches and megachurches. The concept stays the same, but the methods are adapted to meet the needs of the group.

Note From the Author

I hope that this book helps you in your work with junior high students. I know that this concept of "kids reaching kids" works. I've seen it myself. The 6-8th grade kids in my group are doing it now! The stories that they tell are incredible. Not all of them are successes, but most of them are. My prayers are that you will find this helpful to you and your ministry.

how to
share your faith
when you haven't
got a clue

CLUELESS
evangelism

clip-art promo page

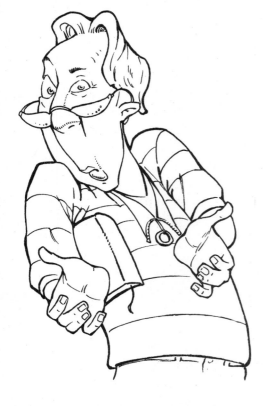

CLUELESS
evangelism

CLUELESS

Junior high students are in the middle of a transition. When they were in elementary school Mom and Dad were their friends. But something strange happens when a student enters junior high. No one has been able to determine the cause of this change (although I believe that it is caused by cafeteria food!). All of a sudden, Mom and Dad are uncool and friends become the number one driving force in the life of the student. Teens will do almost anything to fit into a group. Sometimes this is good, but more often than not, it has a negative effect.

This is more than just another lesson on friendship. Today we want to talk about how your students can make friends with the express purpose of leading them to a relationship with Jesus. Without a doubt, friends are important. Show your students how to be a true friend by introducing their friends to God.

MISSION POSSIBLE: Developing Purposeful Friendships

Lesson Text
Mark 16:15; Luke 15:1-32; John 1:35-42; Acts 1:8

Lesson Focus
Teens can build friendships with the express purpose of leading them into a relationship with Jesus Christ.

Lesson Goals
As a result of participating in this lesson, students will:
• Learn that God desires that each of them show others the way to eternal life.
• Ask God to provide opportunities for them to share what He means to them.
• Select a target person.

1 ◆ Open It Up

♛ IT'S IN THE CARDS

Distribute a deck of playing cards to your group, one card per person. Then call out different combinations, such as: **"Get into groups that add up to 65,"** or **"Find four people of the same suit"** or **"Find three others that are holding the same number as you."** For larger groups, use more than one deck. For smaller groups, take out some cards. Once students are divided into smaller groups have them each share something unique about themselves. After a minute, call out a different combination for which students are to search. (From <u>Play It Again! More Great Games for Groups</u>, by Rice and Yaconelli, Zondervan Publishing, 1993.)

Conclude by saying, **"It's not always this easy to meet new people. Today we're going to be talking about how we can make new friends. We want to develop these friendships for the purpose of introducing others to Jesus Christ."**

Materials needed:
Deck of playing cards

Check This . . .
You may want to use the video from the Newsboys entitled "Shine" or Audio Adrenaline's "AKA Public School" as the students enter the room.

Another introductory song that could be played is "God Is Not a Secret," by the Newsboys, recorded on their release *Take Me to Your Leader.*

Choose from another Open It Up option or go on to the Get Into It section.

♔ ♔ I Lost It

Begin by saying, **"Every one of you has lost something at one time or another. It might have been your keys, wallet, shoes, glasses, retainer or your homework. When you are looking for a lost item, the search usually starts out casually and then quickly escalates to a frantic, all-out tornado through the house."** Invite students to think about the last time they lost something and couldn't find it. Then ask a few of them to tell what they lost and where they found it or didn't find it.

Comment, **"When someone loses something, he puts all of his energy into finding it. Today we are going to talk about lost items, but not keys or homework. We're talking about lost people and how we can help them find God."**

Choose from another Open It Up option or go on to the Get Into It section.

♔ ♔ ♔ Where's Ronald?

Materials needed:
French fries with lots of aroma

Before class, go to a local fast-food restaurant and buy some french fries (McDonald's® has great-smelling fries.). Before your students arrive, hide the fries somewhere in the room. Make sure that the aroma permeates the classroom. When your students enter, someone is sure to comment on the smell. Tell them that the first person to find the fries can eat them.

After they have been located, say, **"The reason that you found the fries was that you recognized their smell and tracked them. Today we are going to talk about how we can search out people that need to know about God and begin a process of leading them into a relationship with Him."**

Continue with the Get Into It section.

 ## ❷ Get Into It

♔ The End of the Earth?!

Materials needed:
Reproducible student sheet on page 13 of this book; colored markers

Have your students read Mark 16:15 and Acts 1:8. Say, **"These verses show us that God wants us to go and tell others about Him. He wants us to go to Jerusalem, Judea, Samaria and to the ends of the earth. What does this mean? Well, Jerusalem was a city, Judea is comparable to your state, Samaria could mean the country and the ends of the earth is self-explanatory."**

Distribute copies of student sheet on page 13 to each student and provide colored markers.

Choose from another Get Into It option or go on to the Take It With You section.

♔ ♔ SEARCHING FOR THE LOST

Hand out copies of the student sheet on page 15. Then have your students look up Luke 15:1-32. Allow them to work in groups (use the same groups if you did the activity "It's in the Cards" earlier). Next to each Scripture, encourage the students to record what was lost, who was looking for it and what happened when it was found.

Conclude this activity by saying, **"In each of these stories there was a celebration when the lost item or person was found. God wants us to search out lost people and find them. When they are saved, there is a heavenly celebration that goes on. Look again at Luke 15:10."**

Choose from another Get Into It option or conclude with the Take It With You section.

Materials needed:
Bibles; reproducible student sheet on page 15 of this book; writing utensils

♔ ♔ ♔ A BRUSH WITH FAME

Begin, **"Some of you have had an opportunity to meet a famous person."** Invite students to tell about their brushes with fame—such as meeting the President of the United States, a professional athlete or the youth minister's mom. Afterward, have your students turn to John 1:35-42 and read it silently.

Ask them to respond to these questions:
- **What famous person did John meet?** *(Jesus.)*
- **What did he do?** *(He followed Him and spent the whole day with Him.)*
- **Then what was the first thing that he did?** *(He went and found his brother Simon and told him about Jesus.)*

Comment, **"Anytime we meet someone famous we can't wait to tell our friends about that experience. It should be the same way when we get to know Jesus. Many times, though, we are not as excited about telling others about our relationship with Jesus as we should be. Why do you think that is the case?"**

Allow students to respond. Write their answers on the chalkboard. They will probably says things like "fear," "we don't know enough," etc. Then have them look at Mark 16:15 and read God's charge for all of us.

Conclude with the Take It With You section.

Materials needed:
Bibles; chalk and chalkboard

3 ◆ Take It With You

♔ BUILDING A FRIENDSHIP

All of your students have friends. Most of them have best friends. If you asked them how they became friends, very few could tell you how. They would say that "it just happened." Say, **"We want to learn how we can build friendships on purpose. Our goal is to introduce these people to Jesus Christ.**

"In his book, <u>Campus Life J. V.</u>, Dave Veerman gives us a simple way to begin a friendship.

It's based on the acronym S.N.I.F.:

'S' = starter statement (*'It sure is hot today!'* or *'Hey, I like your shirt.'*)

'N' = name (*'My name is Fred. What's your name?'*)

'I' = interests (Look for things that each of you like and possibly have in common.)

'F' = family (Ask about their home, brothers, sisters or pets.)

All you have to remember is 'S.N.I.F.' and you're on the way to making a new friend."

Continue with the next option in this section.

♕ ♕ POINT PERSON

Almost everyone knows that God *wants* him to tell his friends about Him, but actually doing it is another thing. Today each of your students is going to choose a "point person." This is the person that they want to "point" toward God and begin the process of leading him or her into a relationship with Him. This is a serious time. Give them a few moments to think about someone they know who does not have a relationship with God.

Spend a few minutes in prayer, some of it silent, asking God to help them identify one person who will be their "point person." Then, distribute two 3" x 5" index cards to each student. Direct them to write down the name of their point person on the cards. One card will serve as a reminder when they take it home.

Using a piece of poster board, attach the second set of index cards to the board and place it on the wall so that everyone can see the names of the point people.

Conclude by saying, **"Today we have talked about building a friendship with someone to lead them into a relationship with God. The goal is not to be manipulative, but to share the best thing in the world. What could be more exciting than to stand before God one day with your point person?"**

Have your students commit to staying loyal to their point person, even if they do not accept God right away.

♕ ♕ ♕ NOT JUST A LOT OF HOT AIR

Sometimes your students make commitments and don't keep them. Their promises are just a lot of hot air. Give each person an empty balloon and a small slip of paper. Ask students to write their point person's name on the paper and insert it into the balloon. Then, have them blow up the balloon and tie it.

Conclude, **"People will ask what the balloon is for and will give you an opportunity to share about this lesson. When the balloon breaks, the point person's name will come out. Keep it as a reminder."**

Materials needed:

3" x 5" index cards (two per student); writing utensils; poster board; masking tape

---

Check This . . .
Group Handstand

Divide students into groups of three. Have one person in each group do a handstand while the other two people support him. While the student is upside down, have the other two quickly pray that he will keep his commitment to God to reach out to his point person. Then, switch roles two more times until everyone has been prayed for.

Materials needed:

Balloon and slip of paper for each student; pencils

---

the end of the earth?!

In Acts 1:8, just before Jesus was taken up into Heaven, He challenged His followers to be His **"witnesses in Jerusalem, and in all Judea and Samaria, and to the ends of the earth."** Jerusalem represents our town, Judea our state and Samaria our country. Mark our city and outline our state. Then color in our country and the rest of the scope of our responsibility (the world).

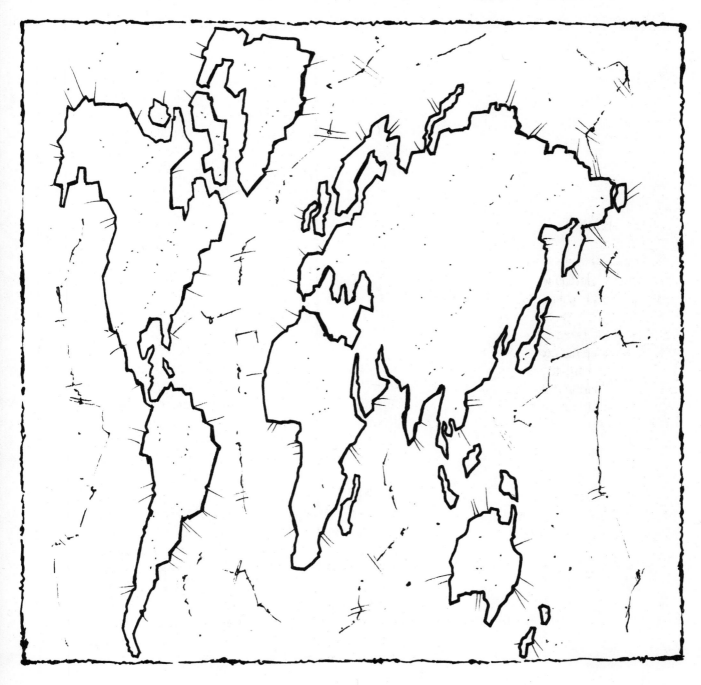

Searching
for the
LOST

Look up Luke 15:1-32 and fill in the chart below:

WHAT WAS LOST?	WHO WAS LOOKING?	WHAT WAS THE RESULT?
Luke 15:1-7		
Luke 15:8-10		
Luke 15:11-32		

PREPARING THE EVIDENCE: Your Testimony

Lesson Text
Mark 5:1-20; 7:31-37; John 4:1-26, 39, 40; Revelation 12:11

Lesson Focus
Students will learn how to write their personal testimony and how to seize the opportunity to share what God means to them.

Lesson Goals
As a result of participating in this lesson, students will:
• Learn the essential components of an effective testimony.
• Write out and practice their testimony on other students in class.
• Take the opportunity to share their testimony with their target person.
• Invite their target person to an outreach event.

Throughout history most of what has been passed down has been by way of spoken communication. People told stories to relay traditions and history to the next generation. Today we use the telephone, fax machine, magazines, radio, TV and many other forms of communication. The power of a good story is incredible. It can still hold the attention of listeners.

Today we do not often tell stories. Yet, the Bible teaches us that part of our walk with God is to tell others about our life with Him. We need to remember what God has done for us and pass it down to the next spiritual generation. Today you and your students will be learning about the effectiveness of a testimony. Sometimes people get nervous about the word "testimony" because of all the pictures that word conjures up—crying in front of the church, yelling and overdramatic stories of conversions. Today your kids will learn that a testimony is, simply, **"the story of my journey with God."**

1 ◆ Open It Up

♔ MY FAVORITE STORY

Before class, think of a story from your life. It might be from a great vacation, a humorous situation or a near-death experience. Tell students to begin thinking of a story of their own that they can tell. While they are thinking, tell your story. Divide your students into pairs and have them share their stories with each other. Allow about five minutes for them to do so. After the time has expired, give several volunteers an opportunity to share their stories.

Conclude this activity by saying, **"Today we are going to be talking about stories. We will discuss stories from the Bible, as well as stories about our own spiritual journey with God."** Choose from another Open It Up option or continue with the Get Into It section.

Check This . . .
As students are entering the room, play a testimony song such as "Secret," by Audio Adrenaline, on their album *bloOm*, or "Love Song for a Savior," by Jars of Clay, on their self-titled debut release.

Materials needed:
A book of nursery rhymes

♕ ♕ Now I Lay Me . . .

Think of your favorite nursery rhyme, Aesop's fable or children's story. At the beginning of class, tell your favorite story (or read it). Then ask students to think about their favorites. Allow about five minutes for students to tell their stories to one another in pairs.

Comment, **"These stories meant a lot to us as children. As junior high students, they are not as cute, but they *do* teach some important lessons. Today we are going to take a look at two different kinds of stories. The first is a biblical story and the second is a personal story or testimony."**

Choose from another Open It Up option or move on to the Get Into It section.

♕ ♕ ♕ What's in a Word?

Say, **"The English language is filled with many peculiarities. Some words have many different meanings."** Say a word to your group and let them come up with as many different meanings as possible. For instance "light" can mean *not heavy, using little force* (hit me lightly), *dizzy* or *giddy* (light-headed), *radiant energy acting on the retina of the eye* (light waves) or *bright*. Other words like this include cool, buzz, stud and bad. If you have time, try some of these out with your students as well.

Comment, **"Today we are going to talk about the word 'testimony.' What do you think of when you hear that word?"** Allow several students to respond. Then, say, **"A testimony can mean the following: (1) giving false testimony means to lie, (2) if someone serves as a testimony, he is a good example and (3) if you give your testimony, you simply tell the story of your spiritual experience."**

Continue with the Get Into It section.

◆ 2 Get Into It

♕ One Day on the Way to the Gerasenes

Materials needed:
Bibles

Have students pantomime Mark 5:1-20. Ask for a few volunteers to act out this scene. There will not be any speaking parts except for the narrator, who will read the text. You will need: Jesus, some disciples, the man with the evil spirits, a large herd of pigs and people from the surrounding towns. Have the narrator read the text and pause for the action to take place.

After the pantomime, thank your participants, then say, **"At first this demon-possessed man was feared by everyone and forced to live in the cemetery. But, after he met Jesus, his life was changed forever. In fact, he went away to the Decapolis (a ten-city region) and told everyone how much Jesus had done for him. All who heard him were amazed!**

"When we meet Jesus, our change isn't quite so dramatic. But we should go and tell others what has happened in our life. This is called our 'testimony.' Although ours may not be quite like this man's, it is still very important."

Choose from another Get Into It option or go on to the Take It With You section.

♔ ♔ MY TOP 10

Your students are probably familiar with David Letterman's "Top 10" lists. Divide them into three groups and assign each group one of the following Scriptures: Mark 5:1-20; Mark 7:31-37; or John 4:1-26, 39, 40. Distribute copies of the student sheet on page 21 of this book. Make sure that each group has a pen or pencil. Instruct them to compose a "Top 10" list that each of the changed people might have come up with—if they had known about Dave Letterman's tradition. For example, the Geresene demoniac's "Top 10 Reasons I'm Glad I Met Jesus" might include statements like, *"It sure beats cutting myself with stones!"* or *"My neighbors in the old neighborhood would never talk to me."*

After they have finished, let a spokesperson from each group read their list aloud to everyone else. Conclude by saying, **"Obviously people in the New Testament never heard of a 'Top 10' list, but their lives were changed in exciting ways. When we come into a relationship with God, our lives are also changed. The things that we used to do that are wrong, we now know we shouldn't do anymore. We want to please God, not ourselves. Let's take a look at how we can tell others, and, more specifically, our point person, about the change God has made in our life."**

Continue with another option in this section or conclude with Take It With You.

♔ ♔ ♔ WHO? WHAT? WHEN? WHERE?

Divide students into three groups and distribute copies of the reproducible student sheet (page 23). Assign each group one of the following Scriptures: Mark 5:1-20; Mark 7:31-37; or John 4:1-26, 39, 40. Direct students to read their assigned Scripture and complete the student sheets within their groups. After five minutes let them report their findings to the rest of the class.

Conclude with Take It With You.

◆3 Take It With You

♔ WHAT IS A TESTIMONY?

Begin by asking, **"How do we communicate today? We use telephones, fax machines, E-mail, TV, magazines,**

Materials needed:
Reproducible student sheet on page 21 of this book; Bibles; writing utensils

Check This . . .

Divide students into groups of three–four and give each group a blank sheet of paper and a pencil. Assign each group one of these texts: Mark 5:1-20; Mark 7:31-37; or John 4:1-26, 39, 40. Have students imagine that they are newspaper reporters who are doing an on-the-scene report about this dramatic story.

Give them five–eight minutes to compose their stories. Then, let them read their reports to the rest of the group. Suggest that they write the story from a different perspective. For example, the Mark 5 account could be written from the viewpoint of the men who had tried to tie and chain the possessed man and had seen him break the chains. Or, the account of the woman at the well could be viewed through the eyes of a nosy neighbor lady who can't believe the difference. Encourage students to be creative!

Materials needed:
Reproducible student sheet on page 23 of this book; Bibles; writing utensils

Materials needed:
Chalkboard and chalk

music, newspapers and signs. But, in biblical times, most of the communication was spoken. Stories were handed down from generation to generation.

"Telling someone what God means to me and what He has done in my life is my 'testimony.' Let's learn the components of a good testimony, write out our testimony and think about sharing it with our point person."

Write the word "testimony" on the chalkboard vertically. Have them make an acrostic using the letters of the word "testimony." Here is a simple example: T—*Telling*; E—*Everyone*; S—*Some*; T—*Truth*; I—*In*; M—*My*; O—*Own*; N—*Nasal*; Y—*Yodel*. The acrostic doesn't have to be grammatically correct, it just needs to describe what a testimony is—my story about what God means to me.

♕ ♕ MY OWN STORY

Comment: **"A testimony is a straightforward description of your life as a Christian. There are some things that make up a strong testimony. First, talk as you would in any normal conversation. This is not a time to preach! Second, talk about how you came to accept Jesus as your Savior. If you don't remember the exact time and place, it's OK. If you grew up in a Christian family, you may have had an idea of God since you were a child. Share when God started to become real in your life. Third, tell how your life is different since you allowed God to be number one. You may want to end with a simple Bible verse that means a lot to you."**

Distribute paper and pens. This activity can take anywhere from 10-30 minutes, depending on your group. Invite students to write their personal stories on the paper. Remind them to use simple phrases and to avoid being overly dramatic.

After they have written out their spiritual story, divide students into pairs and have one person read their story to their partner, then switch roles.

♕ ♕ ♕ NOT JUST BY CHANCE

Your students have each chosen a point person and written out their story. Now they need to begin praying and looking for a simple way to share that story with their point person. If they just leave it to chance, it will never happen. The students need to ask God to provide them with the appropriate opportunity to share their story. God *will* answer their prayers.

Revelation 12:11 assures us that a person's testimony can overcome Satan's powers. If your students are serious about leading their point person to a relationship with Jesus Christ, their story will be a powerful part of that process. Have students remain in their same pairs and pray for each other, asking God to provide the opportunities for them to share their story.

Materials needed:
Blank paper; pens or pencils

Check This . . .
Prayer Memo
Your students will probably want to share their story with their point person, but may be a little apprehensive. Instead of having a closing prayer circle, hand out 3" x 5" index cards and have them write out their prayers in the form of a short note. Urge them to carry this card around in their pocket to remind them about their promise to share their story.

MY TOP 10

Look up your assigned Scripture and focus on the person in this account whose life was dramatically changed. If he or she had been familiar with Dave Letterman's "Top 10" tradition, how would this list have been completed?

TOP 10 REASONS I'M GLAD I MET JESUS

10.

9.

8.

7.

6.

5.

4.

3.

2.

(drum roll, please)

1.

Who? What? When? Where?

Choose one of the following Scriptures: Mark 5:1-20; Mark 7:31-37; or John 4:1-26, 39, 40. Read the verses and answer the questions about the story.

Who?	What happened?
Where?	Where?

Lesson 2   23

Throughout the New Testament there are many instances of Jesus and His disciples talking to individuals about their relationship with God. In many of these situations the people came to Jesus or the disciples and brought up the subject. In today's culture that is not the norm. Teenagers will talk about practically everything with their friends—from sports, to current events, parents to siblings, sex, death and the future. One subject that is rarely discussed is God. Perhaps this is one area that they feel as though they are not experts, or they don't want to offend anyone. In reality, people are dying to learn more about God and the truth. Today your students will discover how to "bridge the gap" in talking to their friends and point person about God.

1 ◆ Open It Up

♛ Big Steps, Baby Steps

This game is very similar to the childhood game of "Red Light, Green Light." If you have a large classroom, gym or outdoor field, choose one end of the area as a starting line and the opposite end as a finish line. Have students stand along the starting line. Choose one person to be "it" and have him stand on the finish line. Facing away from the starting line, he yells one of the following: "big steps," "baby steps" or "stop." If he says, "big steps," everyone moves toward the finish line using giant steps. If he says, "baby steps," they move toward the finish line using little steps. When he says, "stop" and turns around, everyone must freeze. Anyone he sees moving is out and waits until the next round. The first person to cross the finish line is the winner of the round and gets to be "it" for the next round.

Conclude by saying, **"The key to success was choosing to take the right steps at the right time. Today we are going to talk about how we can successfully reach our friends for Christ. We'll talk about taking the appropriate steps."**

Taking the Plunge: Talking to Your Friend About God

Lesson Text
Matthew 19:16-22; Luke 19:1-10; 23:26-43; John 3:1-21; 4:1-26, 39

Lesson Focus
We can learn how to talk to others about a relationship with God by looking at how Jesus did it.

Lesson Goals
As a result of participating in this lesson, students will:
• Discover how Jesus and His disciples talked to people about a relationship with God.
• Evaluate excuses people give for not sharing Christ with their friends.
• Learn how to talk to their point person about God in a nonthreatening and easy way.
• Role-play various situations they could encounter when talking to their point person.

Materials needed:
Large open area, such as a field or gymnasium

Check This . . .
You may want to play the video "Show Me the Way," by John Schlitt, as students are entering the room.
The song, "Space," from the album of the same title, is recorded by the new Christian group, Bleach. It is a great song about friendship evangelism.

Materials needed:

Two chairs—one labeled "The Champion" and the other labeled "The Challenger"

Check This . . .
Super Password

Choose two pair of students. Have each pair sit facing one another. The object of the game is for one person (who knows the answer) to give a one-word clue to his partner (who does not know the answer). Each pair has three seconds to try to give the correct one-word answer. If they give an incorrect answer or no answer, it is the other team's turn. Score 10 points for a correct answer; each time the clue is passed to the other team, deduct one point in value.

An example follows: The word is "apple." The clue giver might say, "fruit." The receiver responds, "banana." That is an incorrect answer, so it passes to the other team and is now worth nine points. The giver says, "red." The receiver would say, "apple," which is correct. Their team would score nine points. Choose from the following words or use some of your own: pizza, TV, family, soccer, math or musician. Make sure that your last word is "God."

Materials needed:

Reproducible student sheet on page 29 of this book; Bibles; writing utensils

Do the other Open It Up option or go on to the Get Into It section.

♛ ♛ HELP! I'M TALKING AND I CAN'T SHUT UP!

Almost every junior high class has several students who love to talk! They will love this activity. In the front of the class, set up two chairs. Label one "The Champion" and the other "The Challenger." Choose several volunteers and have the first two sit in the chairs. Explain the object of this game.

Say, **"Today we will crown someone with the title of *King* or *Queen Conversationalist*. The game will consist of several rounds. Each round will be 30 seconds long. I will mention a subject, and, when I say 'go,' each contestant will discuss that topic for the entire 30 seconds.** (Both people will be talking at the same time. This will provide some great laughs). **At the end of the round the audience will decide who did the best job and the winner will move to the champion's chair. The next volunteer will sit in the challenger's chair, I'll announce another subject and round 2 will begin. We will have several rounds until there is a clear champ."**

Choose several unrelated subjects for the competition. Some possibilities are restaurants, athletes, the mall, school food, God, my favorite book and the importance of friends.

After you have crowned a *King* or *Queen Conversationalist*, say, **"Some people are very good at talking to others—almost *too* good. There are some subjects that we love to talk about. Others aren't so easy. Today we are going to look at how we can talk about God with our friends."**

Move on to the Get Into It section.

Get Into It

♛ CLOSE ENCOUNTERS

Divide students into five groups and give each group a copy of the student sheet on page 29. Begin by asking, **"Have you ever walked down a hallway or through a doorway and met a person coming from the opposite direction and done the 'Sidestep Dance'? You know what I mean: you move to the left, they move in front of you. You move to the right and they accidentally mirror your move. Finally someone takes control and says, 'You first,' and waits until the other person has passed by. When it comes to talking to our friends about God, many times we are stuck in that awkward position of 'dancing' around the subject. Let's take a look at how Jesus responded to some close encounters."**

Assign each group one of the following Scriptures to use in answering the questions: Matthew 19:16-22; Luke 19:1-10;

Luke 23:26-43; John 3:1-21; or John 4:1-26, 39. Give them five minutes to answer the questions. Then have a group representative share their answers with everyone else.

Point out, **"In most of these close encounters the people came to Jesus looking for direction. But in several cases, *He* sought out the people and initiated the conversation."**

Ask students to discuss these questions:

• **Why do you think people came to Jesus?** (Some possibilities include: *He had done miracles, He was a famous person* and *He walked His talk*.)

• **Why do you think that Jesus chose to approach the Samaritan woman and Zacchaeus?** *(They would serve as examples for us. He knew that they were at the lowest point in their lives and that they would be dramatically changed.)*

Conclude by saying, **"Not everyone responded positively to Jesus—such as the rich young ruler and the unrepentant thief on the cross—but that never stopped Jesus from telling others about a relationship with God."**

Do the other Get Into It option or conclude with the Take It With You section.

♛ ♛ EXCUSES, EXCUSES

While students are still in their groups, have them use the back of their student sheets to make a list of excuses that Jesus could have used for *not* talking to their assigned person. For example, concerning Nicodemus, He could have said, *"It's too late; I'm too tired"*; concerning the Samaritan woman, He could have said, *"It's too hot"* or *"I shouldn't talk to that kind of person."* Point out that Jesus never once used an excuse for not telling someone about a relationship with God. In fact, He sought out every opportunity He could to share the message.

Next, give students a few minutes to list excuses *they* have used or have heard others use for not sharing their faith. After two to three minutes have them share their strongest excuses and have an open discussion about the perceived and actual consequences of talking to their friend about God. Lead them to see that most of our excuses are very pitiful.

Conclude with the Take It With You section.

Materials needed:
Reproducible student sheet on page 29 of this book; Bibles; writing utensils

◆ 3 ▸ Take It With You

♛ ACT IT OUT!

Before class, cut out the cards on page 31. Recruit four pairs to act out the situations. In each pair, give one student the "Christian" card and the other the "non-Christian" card. Don't let partners see one another's cards. Both cards give the scenario, but the non-Christian's card also gives some additional help for

Materials needed:
Scenario cards from the reproducible student sheet on page 31 of this book

the response and attitude. The "Christian" will have to be ready for anything, as some unexpected surprises may arrive.

When students are ready, allow them to present their role plays. Afterward, thank your participants and conclude with another Take It With You option.

♛ ♛ OH, THE PLACES WE'LL GO

In today's Scriptures, Jesus chose some unusual places to talk to people about their relationship with God. (On a cross, late at night, at a well and during a parade.) Ask, **"Wouldn't it be great if we could choose the exact time, location and surroundings of when we talk to our point person about God? Sure it would. But if we wait until it is convenient or until everything is perfect, we'll never do it."**

Distribute paper and pencils. Have students draw a vertical line down the paper from top to bottom. Give them a couple of minutes to list, on one side of the paper, all of the places they know they will go this week. On the other side, have them think through the situation and decide whether or not it would be a good place to begin talking about God to their point person.

After a few minutes, have several volunteers tell about their one or two best locations. Say, **"If you're not prepared, you'll never tell your friends about God. Think through where you'll be, who'll be there and what will be going on. When the time comes, you'll be ready for action."**

Close the session by using one of the last two options.

♛ ♛ ♛ FAST-FOOD CLOSING

If you have a small group, or just happen to have a lot of money, go to a local fast-food restaurant and buy enough gift certificates for everyone. Close the session by giving each student a gift certificate and directing students to write the name of their point person on it.

Comment, **"Make it your goal to talk to your point person about God this week. This gift certificate should be used to take him or her out for a soft drink, with the purpose of talking about your relationship with God."**

Close by having each person pray for their point person, asking God to allow them to be successful in sharing their faith.

♛ ♛ ♛ ♛ "POINT" PERSON REMINDER

Before class, cut out little arrows, one for each student. Or you could buy small plastic arrows. Another possibility would be temporary tattoos of little arrows. The arrows serve as a reminder that students are to look for an opportunity to share their story with their "point" person this week. Have everyone get a partner and pray that they will be able to successfully share their story with their point person.

Materials needed:
Blank paper; writing utensils

Check This . . .
Mini-Comic Book

Many junior high students love comic books. If your kids enjoy them, distribute blank overhead transparencies and colored markers. Have students divide the transparency into four quarters and draw a four-scene scenario that illustrates them talking to their point person about what God means to them. After 5-10 minutes, turn on the overhead projector and allow students to share their "mini-comic book of salvation." Challenge them to talk to their point person about God this week.

Materials needed:
Gift certificates from a local restaurant

Materials needed:
Construction-paper or plastic arrows

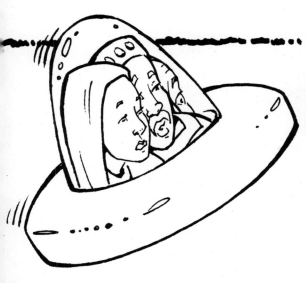

Close Encounters

Scripture:

Who Is Involved?

Who Brought Up the Subject?

What Was the Initial Response?

What Was the Result?

ACT IT OUT!

Cut out these cards and distribute them to the pairs who will be role-playing. Do not let partners see one another's card.

#1 Steve (Christian)

You and Adam sit next to each other in band class. Today after rehearsal you decide to ask Adam about his relationship with God.

#1 Adam (non-Christian)

You and Steve sit next to each other in band class. While walking to your lockers after class, he asks you about your relationship with God. You are very interested and ask him many questions.

#2 Tiffany (Christian)

You and Jessica are good friends. You enjoy going to the mall every Saturday to shop, see a movie, eat and watch people. You decide that today you will ask Jessica a couple of questions about her relationship with God.

#2 Jessica (non-Christian)

You and Tiffany are good friends. You enjoy going to the mall every Saturday to shop, watch a movie, eat and make fun of dumb-looking people who walk by. Today she asks you about God. You call her a hypocrite for laughing at people. You say, "You are no different than I am—why should I change?"

#3 Becky (Christian)

You and John are in the eighth grade and like each other. You have a problem with going out with a non-Christian guy. So you get up the courage to ask John about his relationship with God.

#3 John (Christian)

You have liked Becky for a long time. But you are not sure if she is a Christian. You have a big problem with going out with non-Christians. You are very active in your church youth group and have been a Christian for quite some time.

#4 Greg (Christian)

You and Joe are on the same baseball team at school. Today, after practice, you decide to tell Joe what God means to you.

#4 Joe (non-Christian)

You and Greg are friends, but he seems a little different. He's always talking about God and stuff. You resent it when he brings up the subject to you. In fact, you feel that all Christians are weak and cannot compete in sports. You advise him to quit the team. You leave upset.

Almost any good teacher can present a lesson that will cause students to want to share the gospel with their friends. But, often we fail to give them the tools to do that. Everyone wants to share the gospel—but how? There are many plans and strategies that work. This lesson will help you teach your students a couple of simple methods that have proven to be valid.

Take a little time at the beginning to review what you've taught about choosing a point person, asking some key questions and sharing your testimony. Some students may already have some positive experiences to share. This lesson completes the teaching. A bonus session is provided to help your students bring their non-Christian friends to a non-threatening event. Take a look at this session, beginning on page 43.

GOING ALL THE WAY: Leading Your Point Person to Jesus

Lesson Text

Acts 3:1-10; 4:12-22; 5:17-34; 7:51—8:1; 16:16-38; various verses from Romans

Lesson Focus

With some encouragement, your students can capably lead others into a relationship with Jesus.

Lesson Goals

As a result of participating in this lesson, students will:

• Discover the urgent need that everyone has for a Savior.

• Learn how to lead their friends to Christ.

• Commit to leading their point person to a point where he or she can make a decision for Jesus.

1 Open It Up

♔ DON'T WASTE NO TIME

Begin by saying, **"We never have enough time to do all that we want. We always want more time to sleep, play, watch TV or just relax. In reality, we waste time each day."**

Have students get into groups of four or five and think about all the places that they waste time each day. Distribute a 3" x 5" index card and pencil to each group. Some suggestions are: on the bus, in study hall and waiting in line for lunch. Next, have each group choose one situation in which time is wasted and come up with a list of things they could do to pass the time. These can be as humorous or as serious as they want them to be.

As an example, share the following: **"As an adult, one of the most time-wasting places I encounter is riding on an elevator. Here are some fun things to do on an elevator:**

1. Blow your nose and offer to show the contents of your tissue to other passengers.

2. Whistle the song 'It's a Small World' continuously.

Materials needed:
3" x 5" index cards; writing utensils

Check This . . .

As students arrive, play the song, "Sweet Song of Salvation," by Rebecca St. James. It is recorded on the album *One Way: The Songs of Larry Norman.* Another good choice would be "Love Song," on Third Day's self-titled debut album.

3. Crack open your briefcase or purse, and, while peering inside ask, 'Got enough air in there?'
4. When arriving at your floor, strain to open the doors, then act embarrassed when they open by themselves.
5. Yell 'Chutes away!' whenever the elevator descends.
6. Say 'Ding!' at each floor."

After you have given the groups 5-10 minutes to complete their lists, allow them share them with everyone else. Then say, **"When we put our minds to it, we can come up with several things to do so that we are not wasting time each day. Today we are going to talk about the final step in leading your point person into a relationship with God."**

Do the other Open It Up activity or go on to the Get Into It section.

♕ ♕ SAY WHAT?!

Oxymorons are words that are used together, but have opposite meanings. Some examples include: *jumbo shrimp, light heavyweight, honest crook, pretty ugly, friendly argument, deafening silence* and *black light*. Divide students into groups of four or five and give each group a 3" x 5" card and a pen. Have them come up with their own list of oxymorons. Other examples include: *junk food, alone together, civil war, elementary calculus, lean pork, medium large, military intelligence, second best* and *student teacher*. (Don't read all of these to your students, in case they come up with them on their own.)

Have each group give their top two or three to the others. (You may want to write these down since they could be good.) Close, **"Every day we say things that we really don't mean or that don't make sense when we think about them. Today, we're going to learn how to talk clearly about the most important thing in the world—a relationship with God."**

Go on to the Get Into It section.

⬥ 2 Get Into It

♕ MY DAILY JOURNAL

Begin by saying, **"Most of you know that everyone needs to have a relationship with God in order to have eternal life. The problem is that there is no sense of urgency. Each Christian should be telling others about God's plan for salvation. Let's look at some of Jesus' closest friends and how they made it an imperative to share the good news with those they met. We will consider four people who witnessed the disciples' urgency."**

Distribute copies of the student sheet on page 37. Assign each student one of the following Scriptures to read and then write a journal entry from the perspective of the character mentioned. After a few minutes let students read their entries.

- ACTS 3:1-10; 4:12-22—as told by the court recorder
- ACTS 5:17-34—as told by the captain who retrieved them
- ACTS 7:51–8:1—as told from the perspective of a young Saul
- ACTS 16:16-38—as told from the perspective of the jailer

Allow several students to read their account to the rest of the group. Emphasize that the disciples had an urgency about the message that superseded their circumstances. Say, **"That is also *our* mission—to share the gospel no matter what!"**

Continue with Take It With You or do the other Get Into It option.

♛ ♛ TUBE SOCK THEATER

Provide five or six pairs of clean white socks. Divide students into four groups and assign each group one of today's Scriptures. Give them five minutes to prepare a puppet show depicting their biblical account (using the tube socks as puppets). Let them color faces on their puppets and gather any props needed. Each group will also need a narrator to keep the story moving.

If you have a puppet stage available, use it. If not, use a table with a skirt on the front. This will be a humorous, yet creative, learning experience. After all groups have performed, comment, **"We see from these stories people who wanted to tell others about God's love more than anything in the world. That's the attitude we should also have!"**

Conclude with the Take It With You section.

◆3 Take It With You

♛ BRIDGING THE GAP

Comment, **"Almost everyone has, at one time or another, wanted to tell his friend about God, but did not know where to begin. Jesus used a variety of approaches. Nicodemus came and sought answers from *Him* in John 3. Jesus approached Zacchaeus and invited Himself to lunch at his house. With the thief on the cross, Jesus had a 'captive' audience. There is no one surefire way that will work every time. Here are some ways that *do* work, but we need to pray and ask God to give us wisdom in each situation.**

"When a relationship gets to the point where it is appropriate to bring up the subject, ask a few nonthreatening questions that will guide the conversation. After talking about family or common interests, ask, 'When you go to church, where do you normally go?' This question will not offend anyone. If they attend church regularly, they say so. If they hardly ever go to church, they'll say so. Now you are

Materials needed:
5 or 6 pairs of clean, white socks; magic markers; puppet stage

ready to ask some key questions.

"Ask, 'Do you mind if I ask you a spiritual question?' If they say 'yes,' then the conversation is over. Most likely they will not mind. Ask, 'Do you know for sure that if you died today you would go to Heaven?' If they say 'yes,' ask them why. If they say 'no,' you are ready to share what God means to you and why you want to go to Heaven."

Continue with the next option in this section.

♕ ♕ A Road and a Bridge

Share the following: "After giving your story, your point person will probably have some questions. Here are a couple of approaches that may help as you share your faith." (Distribute copies of the student sheet on page 39.)

The Roman Road

Read Romans 3:23 aloud and explain it. Have students write in their Bible next to 3:23, "6:23." This is their cue to turn to Romans 6:23, read and explain it. Next to Romans 6:23, have them write "5:8." Turn to Romans 5:8, read it, explain it and write "6:12" next to this verse. After Romans 6:12, write 6:3-5. Then they can ask if the person is ready to accept God's free gift of salvation and be baptized.

The Bridge

God created us to praise Him (1 Peter 2:9), to know Him (John 17:26) and to have a satisfying life (John 10:10). Our problem is that sin separates us from God. Everyone who has ever lived has rebelled against Him (Romans 3:23). Sin means that we are cut off from God (Romans 6:23). (Illustrate this by writing the person's name on one side of a piece of paper with the problems "sin and death." On the other side, write "God".) Ask, "What can bring us together with God?" Hard work? No, we can never be perfect. God's remedy is a cross stretching between man and God. God loved us so much that Jesus died for us (John 3:16; Romans 5:8; and 2 Corinthians 5:21).

We can respond by accepting the gift (Ephesians 2:8, 9), repenting, confessing our sins and being baptized (Acts 2:28; Romans 10:9). If we do this, we are assured of salvation (1 John 1:9), have God's Spirit living in us (Acts 2:38) and walk by God's strength (Galatians 2:20; Ephesians 2:10). Conclude with the next activity.

♕ ♕ ♕ Point Person Promise

Distribute copies of the "Point Person Promise." Read through the sheet with students and give them an opportunity to sign their name, the name of their point person, and the date of this covenant. Then, close your time in prayer.

Materials needed:
Reproducible student sheet on page 39 of this book

Check This . . .
Driving the Point Home
From your local hardware store you can purchase enough color-coated nails for each student to have one. (If you can get red nails, these will work best.) Distribute the nails and instruct students to carry them in their pockets to serve as a reminder of the sacrifice that Jesus made for us. It will also serve as a reminder to talk to their "point" person.

Check This . . .
As students are completing their promise, play the song "Did You Mean It" in the background. It is recorded by Third Day on their self-titled debut release.

Materials needed:
Reproducible student sheet on page 41 of this book; writing utensils

My Daily Journal

Many people keep a daily journal or diary. What if you had actually lived during the days of the book of Acts and had recorded what you had seen in your journal? Read the Scripture assigned to you and then write an entry into your daily journal as if you are the person from each story mentioned. Be specific about what you have seen and heard. What is really going on?

Acts 3:1-10; 4:12-22	as told by the court recorder
Acts 5:17-34	as told by the captain who retrieved the apostles
Acts 7:51—8:1	as told from the perspective of a young Saul
Acts 16:16-38	as recorded by the jailer

The Roman Road

1. Romans 3:23—"For all have sinned and fall short of the glory of God."
2. Romans 6:23—"For the wages of sin is death, but the gift of God is eternal life in Christ Jesus our Lord."
3. Romans 5:8—"But God demonstrates his own love for us in this: While we were still sinners, Christ died for us."
4. Romans 6:12—"Therefore do not let sin reign in your mortal body so that you obey its evil desires."
5. Romans 6:3-5—"Or don't you know that all of us who were baptized into Christ Jesus were baptized into His death? We were therefore buried with him through baptism into death in order that, just as Christ was raised from the dead through the glory of the Father, we too may live a new life. If we have been united with him like this in his death, we will certainly also be united with him in his resurrection."

The Bridge

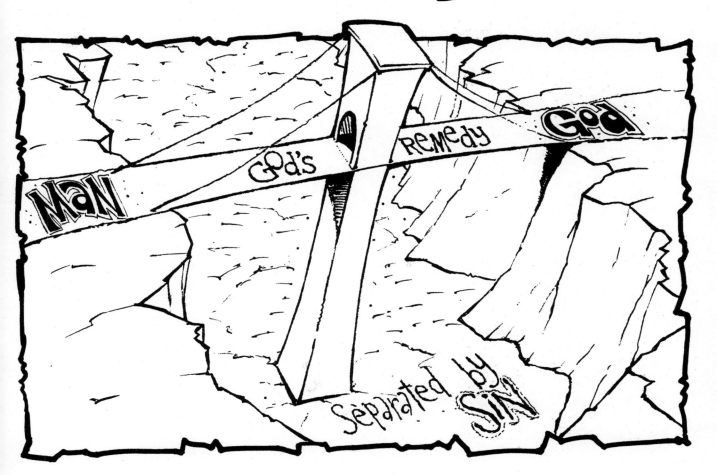

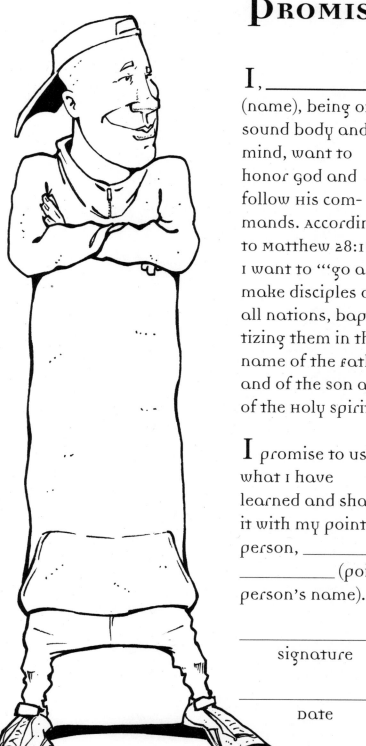

POINT PERSON PROMISE

I, _____ (name), being of sound body and mind, want to honor God and follow His commands. According to Matthew 28:19, I want to "'go and make disciples of all nations, baptizing them in the name of the Father and of the Son and of the Holy Spirit.'"

I promise to use what I have learned and share it with my point person, _____ _____ (point person's name).

_____
signature

_____
date

Outreach Event

Lesson Focus

Provide an opportunity for students to bring their point people to an exciting event.

Lesson Goals

The specific goals of this outreach event are:

• To provide a safe, fun and nonthreatening atmosphere for your students' point people.

• To introduce everyone to the gospel in a simple, clear way.

• To teach everyone a skill that will help them survive junior high life.

• To allow an opportunity for the youth leaders to meet the point people.

• To build community within the group.

This event contains three distinct components: a group activity, a discussion time and a purposeful program. Each of these parts is necessary to accomplish the goals for the event.

The meeting will transition from a very active game time to a more serious time during the program. It can be adapted for a group of any size: from 10-500. Your goal is to provide a place for your students to bring their non-Christian friends. So it should be a safe, nonthreatening atmosphere. This in no way means that the gospel should be compromised or "watered-down." It just will look very different from Sunday morning adult worship!

As you plan, put yourself in the mind-set of an unchurched person. This covers everything from religious jargon to where the bathrooms are located. New kids are judging and evaluating everything, so it is imperative that you make a good first impression. If you do a good job of this, your core students will not hesitate to bring their non-Christian friends again.

1 ▶ Game Time

Junior high students have a ton of energy. Instead of trying to force them to sit in a chair for an hour, direct that energy toward the purpose of the night. Most of the point people coming to this event are not familiar with the church. If they are, their expectations of what will happen may be negative.

The games presented here include options for any size group, from 10-500. ♕ is used for groups of 10-25. ♕♕ is used for larger groups of 26-75 and ♕♕♕ for more than 75.

♕ KING-SIZE VOLLEYBALL

This game is very similar to regular volleyball, with a couple of twists. This game promotes working together as a team—no lone rangers allowed! The rules are as follows:

1. Each team is given a king-size sheet that they will use to

Materials needed:
One volleyball net (or a sheet hung across the room); a volleyball, beach ball or Nerf® soccer ball

Materials needed:

Gym or a large open area; 2-8 volleyballs or Nerf® soccer balls

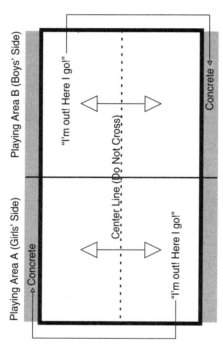

Materials needed:

Open area or gymnasium; whistle; basketballs; a football; playground balls and some imagination

catch and return the ball.

2. Everyone surrounds the sheet, picks it up and moves as one team to catch and return the ball.

3. **No hands or feet** can touch or kick the ball or the other team will get a point and they will get possession of the ball.

4. Points are scored when a team fails to catch or fails to return the ball to the other side.

5. Put a 30-second time limit on returning the ball.

6. The first team to score 15 points wins the game.

♔ ♔ BATTLE BALL ROYALE

The object of this game is to put out the other team's players while keeping your team members "alive." Here are the rules:

1. The game is similar to dodge ball. Each team will attempt to throw the balls and hit the opposing players to get them out.

2. Two different teams will merge to compete together. Guys will play guys and girls will play girls. The guys will stay in one end of the playing area and the girls on the other end.

3. Students are to throw the balls at the opposing players to get them out. They must be hit "on the fly" in order to get out—ricochets do not count! If a player catches the ball, the one who threw the ball is out! If someone is hit on the head, he is not out.

4. Whoever crosses the center line of the playing area is out!

5. When a player is hit on the fly, or fails to make a catch (ricochets do not count), he is out and must go to concrete on the opposite end of the playing area (behind his opposing team).

6. Staying on the concrete, those who are "out" try to get their opponents "out" by throwing balls at them from behind. **Note: they can use only balls that make it to the concrete—they are not allowed to enter the playing field to retrieve one.**

7. If one team is able to completely wipe out the other team, the game is over and they receive 10,000 points.

♔ ♔ ♔ TEAM HYPER CIRCUITS

This game gives everyone a chance to compete and expend tremendous amounts of energy. It includes a series of fast-paced stations in which various teams will line up to successfully complete an activity as many times as possible in the allotted time. At the sound of the whistle, teams will rotate clockwise to the next station. Give 10 points for each successful dunk, throw, goal or basket. Everyone needs to participate, not just the guys!

SLAM DUNK—One at a time, players dribble in and dunk the ball in a lowered rim. No hanging allowed! Score 10 points per dunk.

FOOTBALL THROW—Each person takes a turn throwing from behind a line toward the hoop. Score 10 points per ball thrown through the hoop.

HOCKEY—Shoot from behind a line into the goal taped to a wall for 10 points. No high-sticking allowed!

BANK SHOT—Standing behind a line, each person tries to bounce a ball into a can. Score 10 points per ball bounced in.

2 Discussion Time

Divide students into groups of 10-15. There will need to be one or two adults per group. The purpose of this time is to allow kids to interact with the topic of the night. All day long they have been told to sit down and be quiet in school. We want to ask their opinion, something that adults rarely do. Welcome everyone to the program, introduce any new students and discuss the topic. You will need 15-20 minutes for this time. The topic is "How to Be Honest." Use the following to lead discussion:

1. FACT OR FICTION

Form pairs of students who don't know each other very well. Let them take turns telling their partners one true and one false fact about themselves. Then, let their partner guess which fact is true and which is false. Have them switch partners and repeat the process. Let them keep track of the number of times they guessed correctly during the game. Then, the person with the most correct guesses can share his secrets with everyone.

2. WHOM DO YOU KNOW?

Ask these questions: **"Do you know anyone from the past who was known for his or her honesty? Who (from history) was known for dishonesty? What were some of the things about these people that made them honest or dishonest?"**

3. A LIE

Ask: **"When have you lied to one of your friends, parents or teachers? What did you lie about? Why did you lie to them about this one thing? What were the consequences of lying to these people when and if they found out? When were *you* last lied to? What happened?"**

4. A TRUTH

Ask, **"Can you remember when you came to understand what the truth is? Who has influenced you the most to understand the difference between right and wrong?"**

5. HONESTY MATTERS

Discuss the following: **"Why is it important to tell the truth? What happens to you when you are dishonest? Do you become a stronger or weaker person? How could we help people become more honest?"**

3 Program

This portion of the event should be held in your normal meeting room. You will transition from a more active focus to a short teaching that challenges students to be honest. This program is flexible, depending on your kids and the availability of

---

Check This . . .

One more idea for a Hyper Circuit station:

Use skateboards and children's plastic bowling pins for human bowling. Have one student push another person (who is on a skateboard) toward the pins. Then, have them set the pins back up and allow the next pair to go.

audio/visual equipment. A sample program for the night is provided below. Included are time estimates, program ideas and supplies needed. It can be done simply with a room and a tape player, or with a sound system, video projection unit and theater lighting. The key to success is to be creative with your resources!

TIME	PROGRAM IDEA	MATERIALS NEEDED
5 minutes	Opening music or video—"Jesus Is Still Alright," by dcTalk, "Truth," by Dakota Motor Company or "New Americans," by Geoff Moore and the Distance	TV/VCR, Video Projection Unit, CD or tape
5 minutes	Announce the scores from "Hyper Circuits"—Play music in the background	"Sirius" CD on Alan Parsons project, EYE IN THE SKY or a song from ESPN's JOCK JAMS or JOCK ROCK
3 minutes	Welcome to the event and giveaway	tape, CD or T-shirt for a prize
5 minutes	Lead a group game of "Simon Says." Make the point that we need to listen to what people say	
5 minutes	Present the drama, "The Test"	students prepared to do skit
2 minutes	Focus time—remind students of tonight's topic and lead in a simple prayer to focus everyone	
15 minutes	Simple lesson on honesty by youth leader	
5 minutes	Play exit music such as "Show Me the Way," by John Schlitt or "Truth and Consequences," by The Newsboys.	CD or tape player; exit music

Check This . . .
Concerning the concept of people's perceptions of what's right, check out some of the facts in Josh McDowell's book, Right From Wrong.

"HONESTY MATTERS" LESSON OUTLINE
Introduction: Tell about a time when you were either honest or dishonest and the outcome. Then point out that everyone in the world has his own concept of what's right.

1. WHAT IS TRUTH? HOW CAN WE TEST TO SEE IF SOMETHING IS TRUE?
One of these statements is true: (1) Truth is defined by God or (2) Truth is defined by man. Webster's dictionary defines truth as "being exactly like the original." Show your driver's license. It used to be an exact copy of you, but now you look very different. Thank goodness! If truth is defined by man, it will change. But, if truth is defined by God, it will never change!

2. WHY SHOULD WE BE HONEST? WHAT IS OUR MOTIVATION?
Everyone has a different answer to this question: *"Mom and Dad say to be honest,"* but not everyone's parents taught them that. *"So you don't get in trouble,"* but if you don't get caught, is it wrong? *"It is just wrong!"* Why? *"It just is."* But why?

Say, **"Because of who God is. He is 100% honest and has never broken a promise."** Share the fact that God kept His word to save the world through His Son Jesus. Therefore, **"God wants us to be honest, because He is 100% truth."**

Conclusion: Tell about someone who was honest because he wanted to be like God. Challenge students to make it *their* goal to be an exact copy of God and they'll be honest people.

THE TEST

CHARACTERS

MARY: one of the girls
AMY: one of the girls
SARAH: the one who pauses the skit
JESSICA: a girl who struggles with cheating on her homework
LIZ: a girl who doesn't want to cheat and is tempted to do so

MARY: How are you guys?
GIRLS: Great! We're fine.
JESSICA: Did you all get your homework done for Mr. Smith's class today?
AMY: Yes I did. I got the answers from Susan.
LIZ: Amy, what's wrong with you? Don't you think you should get the answers on your own?
(The girls laugh)
MARY: Yeah, right!
AMY: Everyone does it, Liz . . . calm down.
LIZ: Well, listen, I've got to get to class. I'll see you later, OK?
(The girls who are good friends with Liz say "bye" and then get into a huddle.)
JESSICA: *(to Amy)* What'dya get for number 4?
(The girls begin to write down the answers feverishly.)
MARY: How about number 3?
JESSICA: What did Susan have for number 5?
MARY: How about numbers 6, 7 and 8?
(The girls, still copying and huddled together, move offstage.)
JESSICA: Let's see 10 through 25!

(Someone crosses the stage with a sign that says "One Week Later.")
JESSICA: Hey Liz. How ya doin'?
LIZ: Great, thanks. I'm sitting here trying to finish my homework for Mrs. Martin's class. Doesn't she realize we have other things to do besides this stupid algebra?!
JESSICA: Really! I know exactly what you mean. I have homework in other classes too! And then, Mrs. D + UM + B = DUMB Martin has to pile on 50 algebra problems with two minutes left in class.
LIZ: I get tired of it, too. Well, I guess it doesn't help to complain. At least that's what my Dad says. "If you just keep at it, it doesn't take too long."
JESSICA: Say, Liz, do you have number 12 done? I just can't figure it out.
LIZ: *(very hesitantly)* Yeah, I've got it done.
JESSICA: Well . . . what'dya get?
LIZ: You know I don't like to give out answers, Jessica.
JESSICA: What's the big deal? I don't get it. *Everybody* borrows answers!
LIZ: You mean *steals* answers!
JESSICA: Listen, we're in junior high now. We're past that "don't look on my paper" stage in our education. Besides, if you were a cool friend you'd give me the stupid answers and we could get on with talking about other . . . important . . . things.
(At this point Sarah runs up from where she is seated in the audience on the front row and turns to the audience. Liz and Jessica freeze and Sarah says . . .)
SARAH: Liz is very tempted to give in and give Jessica the answers to get the copycat off her back. Is it really a big deal? Let's see what Liz decides to do.
LIZ: Jessica, can I ask you a question?
JESSICA: Yeah. Go ahead.
LIZ: Have you honestly thought about number 12? How much time have you spent on it?
JESSICA: A . . . a . . . a . . . I just opened my book. I haven't really tried at all.
LIZ: Listen, Jessica, you're smart. You can do this. It's just that you're not even trying! Why don't we work together on number 12 and any other ones that you have a problem with tonight over the phone?
JESSICA: So, you'll help me?
LIZ: Yeah, of course! We'll find out the answer together. The only answer I'll give you is this . . .
JESSICA: What's that?
LIZ: Honesty is the best answer!